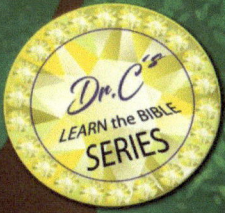

A is for Adam

Author: Dr. C. White-Elliott

Illustrated by: Ariel

www.clfpublishing.org
909.315.3161

Illustrations by Ariel.

ISBN # 978-1-945102-40-0

Printed in the United States of America.

This book is dedicated to

Kingston Jeremiah White

"And the LORD God formed man of the dust of the ground, and breathed into his nostrils the breath of life; and man became a living soul" (Genesis 2:7).

"And the LORD God planted a garden eastward in Eden; and there he put the man whom he had formed" (Genesis 2:8).

*"And out of the ground the L*ORD *God formed every beast of the field, and every fowl of the air; and brought them unto Adam to see what he would call them: and whatsoever Adam called every living creature, that was the name thereof"* (Genesis 2:19).

Adam named the cows and the horses.

Adam named the birds of the air.

Adam named the kangaroo and ostrich.

Adam named the bear and koala.

Adam named the dog and cat.

Adam named the chicken and rooster.

Adam named the different types of fish.

Adam named the reptiles.

Adam named all the animals.

www.ingramcontent.com/pod-product-compliance
Lightning Source LLC
Chambersburg PA
CBHW041958100426

42813CB00019B/2918